FOCUS ON
DINOSAURS

MICHAEL BENTON

SHOOTING STAR PRESS

INTRODUCTION

Dinosaurs were some of the most successful animals of all time. Most of them were large, they all lived on land, and they ruled the Earth for over 160 million years. The first dinosaur bones were named in 1824, and since then hundreds of species have come to light in all parts of the world. Many myths and legends have been told about the dinosaurs. Some are based on fact, others are no more than guesswork. Scientists, however, have been able to find out a great deal about dinosaurs: what they looked like, how they moved, what they ate, how they took care of their young, and even what noises they made. This book tells the story of how all this was discovered and reveals the truth about dinosaurs.

This edition produced in 1996 for
Shooting Star Press Inc
230 Fifth Avenue
Suite 1212
New York, NY 10001

Design	David West Children's Book Design
Designer	Steve Woosnam-Savage
Series Director	Bibby Whittaker
Editor	Suzanne Melia
Picture research	Emma Krikler
Illustrators	George Thompson
	Dave Burroughs

© Aladdin Books Ltd 1993

Created and produced by
Aladdin Books Ltd
28 Percy Street
London W1P 9FF

First published in the
United States in 1993 by
Gloucester Press

ISBN 1-57335-538-0

Printed in Belgium

Geography
The symbol of the planet Earth indicates panels that contain geographical information. These include a world map of dinosaur finds and evidence of dinosaur migration found by looking at trackway sites.

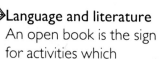

Language and literature
An open book is the sign for activities which involve language and literature. Refer to these sections to learn more about dinosaur science fiction and to discover what dinosaur names really mean.

Science

The microscope symbol indicates where scientific information is given. For example, one panel explains where you can find fossils, and another discusses how the principles of engineering can help to understand how dinosaurs worked.

History

The sign of the scroll and hourglass shows where historical information is given. These sections investigate the first dinosaur finds and take a look at what happened during the great American "Bone Wars."

Math

A ruler and compass indicate math activities. These projects improve knowledge of dinosaurs and math. For instance, you can calculate how much a dinosaur weighed using a scale model and a container of water.

Arts, crafts, and music

The symbol showing art tools signals arts, crafts, or musical activities. These include a discussion of how dinosaur models are built for animation, and which artists are famous for painting dinosaurs.

CONTENTS

BEFORE THE DINOSAURS

The Earth had already passed through most of its history before the dinosaurs appeared. Earth is about 4,600 million years old, and the first dinosaurs came on the scene 230 million years ago. The first living things were tiny creatures, like viruses or bacteria, which lived in the warm oceans 3,500 million years ago. Their fossils can only be seen through a microscope. Larger plants and animals arose 1,000 million years ago, and familiar forms, like shellfish, corals, and fish, existed by 500 million years ago. Fish were the first animals with backbones, and they gave rise to land-living amphibians 375 million years ago, and reptiles a little later. The reptiles ruled the Earth from 275 million years ago until mammals became dominant over 65 million years ago.

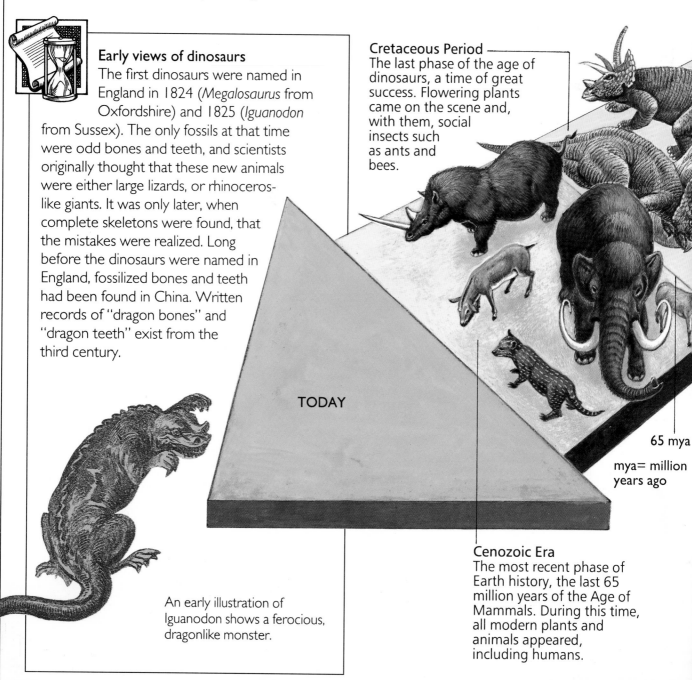

Early views of dinosaurs
The first dinosaurs were named in England in 1824 (*Megalosaurus* from Oxfordshire) and 1825 (*Iguanodon* from Sussex). The only fossils at that time were odd bones and teeth, and scientists originally thought that these new animals were either large lizards, or rhinoceros-like giants. It was only later, when complete skeletons were found, that the mistakes were realized. Long before the dinosaurs were named in England, fossilized bones and teeth had been found in China. Written records of "dragon bones" and "dragon teeth" exist from the third century.

Cretaceous Period
The last phase of the age of dinosaurs, a time of great success. Flowering plants came on the scene and, with them, social insects such as ants and bees.

TODAY

65 mya

mya= million years ago

An early illustration of Iguanodon shows a ferocious, dragonlike monster.

Cenozoic Era
The most recent phase of Earth history, the last 65 million years of the Age of Mammals. During this time, all modern plants and animals appeared, including humans.

It is hard to understand the huge amounts of time involved in the history of life on Earth. When you remember that the first cars ran on the roads only 100 years ago, think how much can happen in spans of millions of years. This chart shows some of the main divisions of geological time over the past 400 million years, and some of the common backboned animals.

Devonian Period
Fish were abundant, and amphibians appeared.

Carboniferous Period
Amphibians, like bloated crocodiles, were the common backboned animals. They lived in warm coal swamps.

360 mya

Permian Period
A drier time in many parts of the world, and ruled by various kinds of reptiles.

286 mya

245 mya

208 mya

Triassic Period
Dinosaurs arose halfway through this time, about 230 million years ago.

Dating rocks
Layers of rock can be placed in order by looking at the fossils in them. But, the exact ages, in millions of years, are worked out by studying the radioactive decay of rock particles. When the elements that made up the Earth were formed, all possible particles were present. Now, the older the rock is, the more the radioactive elements have decayed. It is possible, therefore, to give an age to rocks by looking at the rates of radioactive decay.

144 mya

Jurassic Period
The age of the giant dinosaurs, the great long-necked plant-eaters. Also time of origin of the birds.

Geological periods
The units of geological time were named during the 19th century. The names reflect something of the life at the time, or commonly refer to a part of the world. The main units are the eras: Paleozoic (ancient life), Mesozoic (middle life), and Cenozoic (recent life). The Mesozoic Era, the Age of Reptiles, includes three periods: the Triassic, Jurassic, and Cretaceous. Triassic (three parts) refers to the three main divisions of rocks of that age in Germany. Jurassic was named after the Jura Mountains in Germany, and Cretaceous is based on "Creta" (chalk), a common rock of that particular age in history.

Rock strata

DINOSAUR DIVERSITY

Over 300 species, or kinds, of dinosaur have been named over the past 175 years. These species can be divided up into six or seven main groups. There are the meat-eaters, the *Theropoda*, and the large long-necked plant-eaters, the *Sauropoda*. Together, these two groups form the *Saurischia* ("lizard-hipped" dinosaurs). All other dinosaurs fall into the group *Ornithischia* ("bird-hipped" forms), all of which were plant-eaters. These include the *Ornithopoda*, the two-legged dinosaurs, and the *Ceratopsia*, the horn-faced dinosaurs. The other ornithischians are the armored *Stegosauria*, with plates and spines along their backs and tails, and the *Ankylosauria*, with heavy body armor, armored skulls, and club tails.

Dinosaur crazy

The first dinosaur craze happened in the 1850s in England. At that time, only five or six species of dinosaur were known, but people wanted to know much more. The newspapers and popular magazines were full of all the latest scientific theories. The first dinosaur scenes were painted, and some appeared as posters. Sir Richard Owen and the artist Waterhouse Hawkins created some life-sized dinosaur models that were exhibited in London in 1853. They caused a sensation, and people stood in line for hours to see them. The models were made of concrete and painted in bright colors. They can still be seen in Crystal Palace Park in London.

A Crystal Palace dinosaur

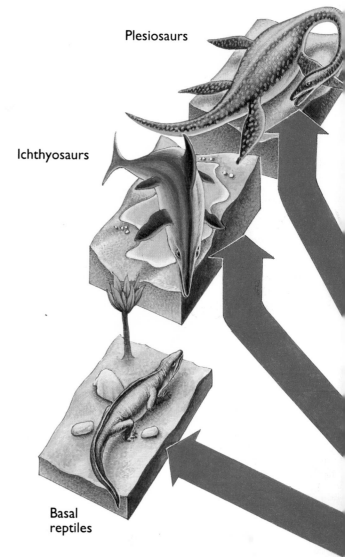

Plesiosaurs

Ichthyosaurs

Basal reptiles

The first reptile group to rule the Earth were the mammal-like reptiles which later gave rise to the true mammals. Successful dog-sized meat-eaters existed during the Permian period.

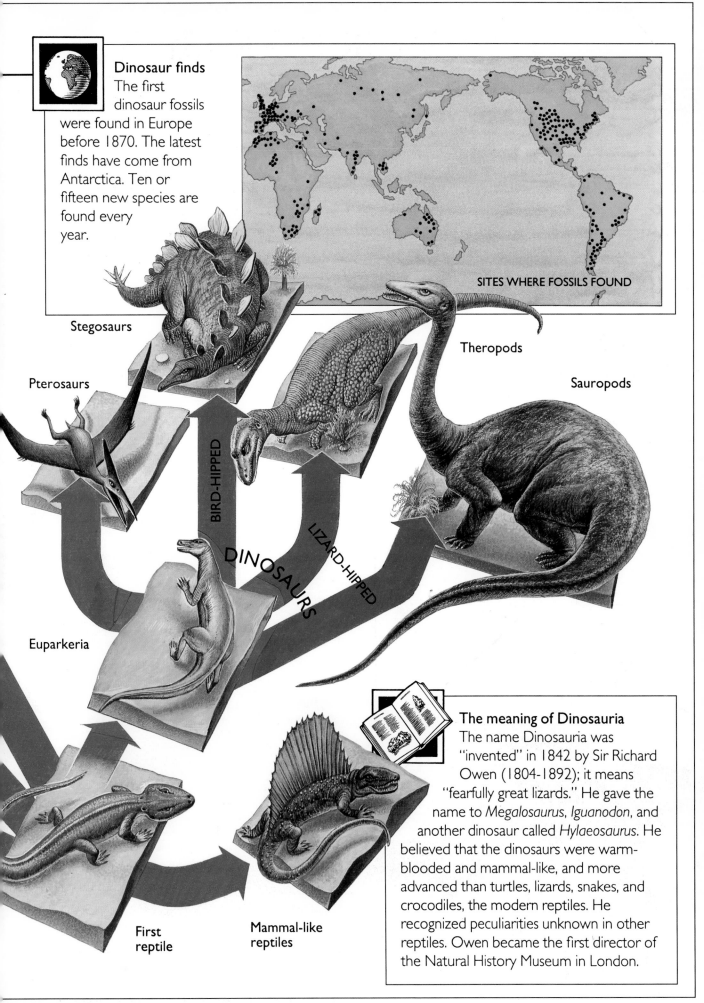

Dinosaur finds
The first dinosaur fossils were found in Europe before 1870. The latest finds have come from Antarctica. Ten or fifteen new species are found every year.

SITES WHERE FOSSILS FOUND

Stegosaurs

Theropods

Pterosaurs

Sauropods

BIRD-HIPPED

LIZARD-HIPPED

DINOSAURS

Euparkeria

First reptile

Mammal-like reptiles

The meaning of Dinosauria
The name Dinosauria was "invented" in 1842 by Sir Richard Owen (1804-1892); it means "fearfully great lizards." He gave the name to *Megalosaurus*, *Iguanodon*, and another dinosaur called *Hylaeosaurus*. He believed that the dinosaurs were warm-blooded and mammal-like, and more advanced than turtles, lizards, snakes, and crocodiles, the modern reptiles. He recognized peculiarities unknown in other reptiles. Owen became the first director of the Natural History Museum in London.

DINOSAUR HABITATS

A great deal is known about the lands in which the dinosaurs lived. Dinosaur fossils are found in rocks, and these rocks can give us some idea of what their world was like: how hot it was, whether it rained or not, how far the land was from the sea, what the plants were like, and what other kinds of animals lived at the same time. These clues come from the study of the *geology* of dinosaur sites; that is, everything that can be learned from the rocks. A geologist who finds fossil mud cracks near a dinosaur skeleton will know that there must once have been pools of water drying out. If a geologist finds some fossil leaves or small shells or fish mixed up with the dinosaur bones, these plants and animals must have been living at the same time, perhaps in a pond where the dinosaur died while drinking.

How fossils formed

Fossils are the remains of plants or animals that once lived on the Earth. Dinosaur fossils are usually odd bones or whole skeletons. After a dinosaur dies (1), the flesh rots or is eaten away. Only the hard bones are left, and mud and sand may be washed around the skeleton, covering it over. Then, after millions of years, the mud and sand may turn into rock, and the spaces in the bone become filled with heavy minerals (2). Later, the fossil bones may be found buried deep in the rock or exposed at the surface.

Continental drift

The continents have not always been where they are now. In fact, all of the continents were joined together during the Age of Dinosaurs. This meant that plants and animals could move all over their world without having to cross great oceans. It was about 100 million years ago that the Atlantic Ocean began to open up.

Present-day

100 million years ago

200 million years ago

50 million years ago

The Jurassic period was a time of high rainfall and lush, tropical conditions. Plant groups of all kinds spread, and huge forests of conifers were established. This climate and vegetation were favorable to dinosaurs, and it was during this time that the gigantic sauropods first appeared.

Collecting fossils

Everyone can collect fossils. Find out from your local museum or library where your nearest fossil sites are. These may be coastlines where there are rocks on the beach, or old quarries. Fossils are found in sandstone, mudstone, or limestone. Be sure to check whether you may go onto the land. Also, take grown-ups with you, since many old quarries and cliffs are very dangerous.

PLANT-EATERS

Most dinosaurs were plant-eaters. These included the long-necked, long-tailed sauropods, which were the biggest land animals of all time; they could grow up to 20 times the size of an elephant! Then there were the armored dinosaurs: the plate-backed stegosaurs (see pages 18-19), the bone-headed pachycephalosaurs, the horn-faced ceratopsians, and the armored ankylosaurs. Some of these may have looked extremely fierce, but they were plant-eaters. The two-legged ornithopods, like *Iguanodon* and the crested, duckbilled dinosaurs, also ate plants and leaves from bushes and trees; this is called browsing. They did not graze since there was no grass. Grasses came on the scene only 25 million years after the dinosaurs had died out.

Iguanodon
The second dinosaur to be named was *Iguanodon*, in 1825. Mary Ann Mantell found some teeth of a plant-eating dinosaur in Sussex, England in 1822. Later, her husband, Gideon Mantell, found more bones and realized that they all came from the same animal. He thought the teeth looked like those of an iguana, a modern plant-eating lizard, even though they were 100 times bigger! So, he invented the name *Iguanodon*, which means "iguana tooth."

Teeth
Plant-eating dinosaurs had a variety of kinds of teeth. The giant sauropods like *Apatosaurus* had long pencil-shaped teeth with sharp edges, useful for cutting large quantities of soft leaves. Most of the armored dinosaurs, like *Ankylosaurus*, had leaf-shaped teeth with zigzag cutting edges, specialized for chewing tougher leaves.

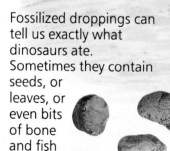

Fossilized droppings can tell us exactly what dinosaurs ate. Sometimes they contain seeds, or leaves, or even bits of bone and fish scales.

Stegoceras

Dinosaur biomechanics

One of the best ways to understand how dinosaurs worked is to think of them like buildings or machines. *Paleontologists* (people who study fossils) may use the principles of engineering in their studies. For example, the huge sauropods had skeletons built like suspension bridges. The massive belly was held up by great ropelike ligaments, fixed to the high spine over the shoulders and hips.

Suspension bridge

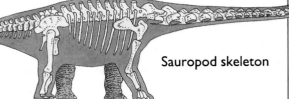

Sauropod skeleton

Apatosaurus

Protoceratops

Ankylosaurus

Bleak House

Charles Dickens (1812-1870), the famous Victorian novelist, included dinosaurs in his *Bleak House*, published in 1853. Dickens wrote of meeting "a Megalosaurus, forty feet long or so, waddling like an elephantine lizard up Holborn Hill" in London. This was the same year that Richard Owen's life-sized dinosaur models were exhibited in London. Dickens was a newspaper reporter earlier in his career and his books were noted for their social commentary and use of current themes of the time.

MEAT-EATERS

The meat-eating dinosaurs all belonged to the group Theropoda, relatives of the large plant-eating sauropods. Theropod means "beast foot" on account of the very sharply clawed, three-toed feet of these animals. The meat-eaters ranged in size from tiny *Compsognathus*, which was only 23 inches long and as tall as a chicken, to the fearsome *Tyrannosaurus rex*. *T-rex* was 39 feet long, and weighed between 6 and 7 tons, even more than an elephant! When *T-rex* opened its mouth, its huge jaws gaped more than 3 feet and it could have swallowed a human being whole! Small theropods fed on lizards and frogs, while larger ones preyed on the plant-eating dinosaurs. Some believe that modern birds may be relatives of the theropods.

The "first" dinosaur

People must have dug up dinosaur bones for many years before *paleontologists* (fossil experts) realized what they were. For example, one early scientist, Robert Plot, thought his dinosaur fossil came from a giant human being. In 1677, he published a book called *The Natural History of Oxfordshire* with a picture of a dinosaur bone. Plot realized it was a part of the thighbone from just above the knee joint, but it was only 150 years later that scientists realized what kind of animal it came from. More bones of this kind of animal came to light near Oxford, and in 1824, Dean William Buckland named them *Megalosaurus*, meaning "big lizard." This meat-eater was the first dinosaur ever to be named.

A modern view of Megalosaurus

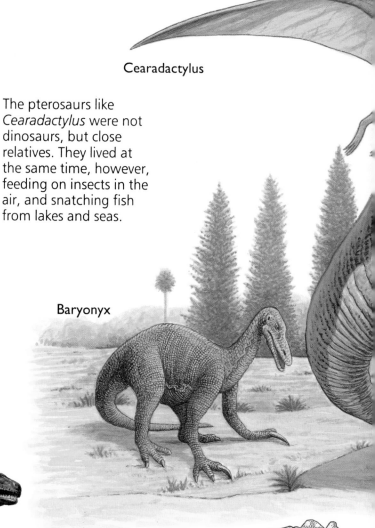

Cearadactylus

The pterosaurs like *Cearadactylus* were not dinosaurs, but close relatives. They lived at the same time, however, feeding on insects in the air, and snatching fish from lakes and seas.

Baryonyx

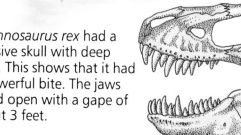

Tyrannosaurus rex had a massive skull with deep jaws. This shows that it had a powerful bite. The jaws could open with a gape of about 3 feet.

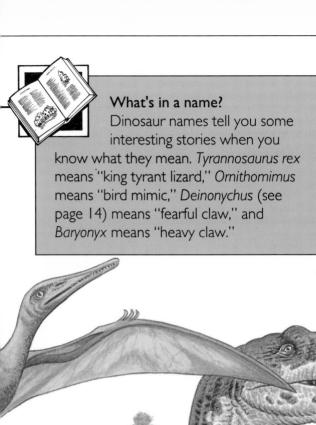

What's in a name?
Dinosaur names tell you some interesting stories when you know what they mean. *Tyrannosaurus rex* means "king tyrant lizard," *Ornithomimus* means "bird mimic," *Deinonychus* (see page 14) means "fearful claw," and *Baryonyx* means "heavy claw."

Dinosaur memorabilia
The first dinosaur craze happened in Britain in the 1850s. Since then the popularity of dinosaurs has spread worldwide. There have been dozens of dinosaur books, TV shows, and newspaper articles. You can buy all kinds of dinosaur things: models, pencils, T-shirts, hats, posters, buttons, and even pasta shapes. See how many dinosaurs items you can collect. What do you think it is about dinosaurs that makes them so popular?

Animated model of *Tyrannosaurus rex*

Allosaurus

Ornithomimus velox

Allosaurus was a typical large theropod, and it probably fed on other dinosaurs, using its huge feet and massive jaws to kill them. *Baryonyx* may have fed on fish, using its long crocodile-like jaws to snap them up. It had a huge hooklike claw which may also have been used to scoop fish from the water. *Ornithomimus* was lightly built, and hunted small animals; it had no teeth in its beaklike jaws and may have been omnivorous.

RUNNING AND SWIMMING

A lot of people imagine that dinosaurs plodded along at an extraordinarily slow pace. It is probably true that the giant plant-eating sauropods could only walk fairly slowly; if one of them had broken into a run, it would have fallen over or broken its bones. The medium-sized plant-eating ceratopsians (see pages 24-25), however, may have trotted quite fast, just like modern rhinos. Some of the smaller meat-eaters could even have run as fast as a racehorse, especially *Ornithomimus* and the vicious *Deinonychus*. But how do paleontologists know how dinosaurs could run and swim when they all died out so long ago? And how can they tell how fast they could run?

Deinonychus

Modern animals use different ways of moving at different speeds. A horse can walk, trot, canter, and then gallop, as it moves faster and faster. Normally, the four legs move in pairs on opposite corners of the horse, but when galloping, both front legs and both hind legs move as pairs together. Some smaller dinosaurs may have been able to gallop, but most could only walk and trot, and the biggest could only walk.

Deinonychus was found in Wyoming, in the 1960s. It was only 10-13 feet long, but it had a huge toe claw that may have been used for slashing at plant-eaters.

Some of the best swimmers were the ichthyosaurs, which were not dinosaurs. These reptiles had powerful tails for swimming, and paddles for steering.

Ichthyosaurus

Evidence

When a dinosaur moved over damp mud or sand, it left footprints. These could then be covered with more sand which preserved the tracks. Fossil dinosaur footprints have been found all over the world. These can show which dinosaur made the track, where it was going, and how fast it was moving.

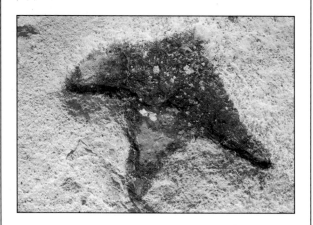

Migration

Recently, paleontologists have found some dinosaur footprint sites where there are thousands of separate trackways. In some cases, the tracks all head in the same direction, and appear to have been made by small and large animals of the same species. These trackways seem to be evidence that there were great herds of dinosaurs marching over long distances. Perhaps they were migrating in search of food or to find warmer winter climates.

These footprints show how the animals walked and how their legs were held. The mammal-like reptile (1) was a sprawler; a dinosaur ancestor (2) walked partly upright; the theropods (3) walked upright on two legs; and the ornithopod (4) could use all fours or walk upright.

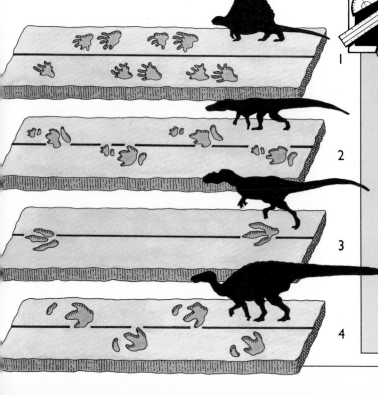

Calculating dinosaur speeds

The faster you run, the longer your strides become. You can test this by walking slowly, walking fast, and then running across some sand. Cover the same distance each time and figure out your various speeds by using a stopwatch. Now measure the distance between each footprint and plot your speed against your stride length. Scientists can calculate dinosaur speeds in this same way by looking at the spacing of their footprints. The wider apart the dinosaur tracks appear, the faster they must have been traveling. If the footprints are very close together, it's likely that they were walking along quite slowly.

PROBLEMS OF SIZE

The most obvious thing about dinosaurs is their size: they were all big. Even though some, like *Compsognathus*, were no bigger than chickens, there is no doubt that dinosaurs lived at a different scale from the mammals. The mammals, the hairy backboned animals like mice, cats, horses, and humans, are said to rule the Earth today. However, the largest living mammal today, the elephant, is a mere midget at 5 tons, compared to the sauropod dinosaurs, many of which weighed from 50 to 100 tons. Most mammals are actually very small – think of mice, rats, shrews, voles, bats, and hedgehogs – and no dinosaur was ever as small as that!

What is the biggest size that a dinosaur could have reached? Could they have reached 200 tons, 500 tons, 1,000 tons? There is a limit for land-living animals caused by the fact that they must be able to lift their great weight on their legs and move. Beyond about 140 tons, a dinosaur would have needed such thick legs to hold up its body weight that it could not have moved at all.

The depth of dinosaur footprints shows how heavy these animals were.

Tyrannosaurus rex

Iguanodon

Weighing dinosaurs

Use a scale model of a dinosaur to calculate how much it would have weighed. Lower the model into a container of water and measure how much is displaced. This is the volume. If the model is to a scale of one-twentieth, the volume is multiplied by 20 x 20 x 20, giving the dinosaur's volume. Living reptiles are 0.9 times as heavy as their volume of water, so multiply by 0.9, to give the weight in grams.

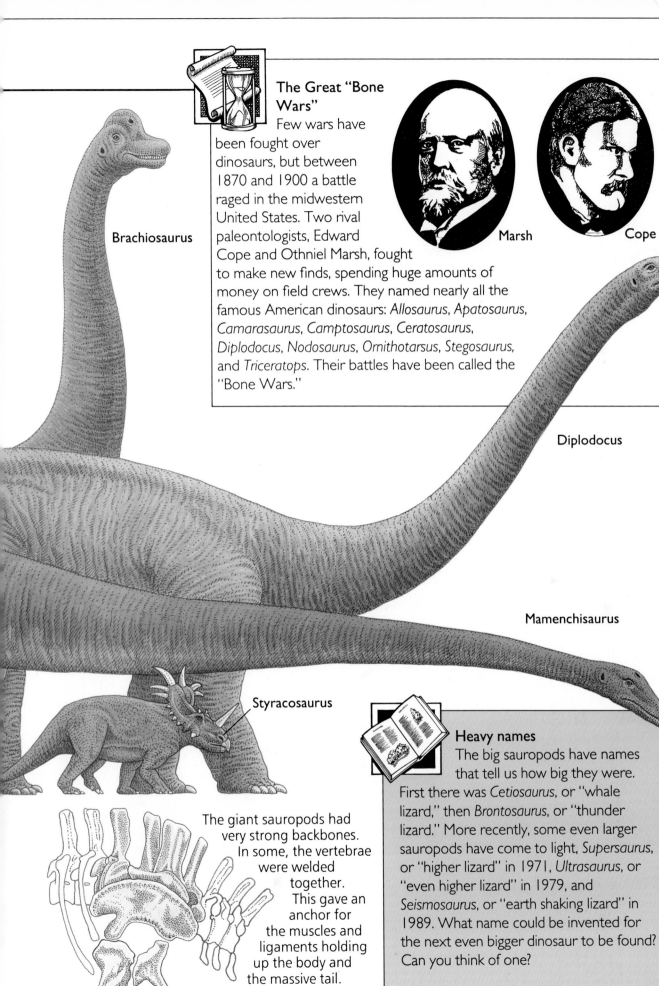

Brachiosaurus

The Great "Bone Wars"

Few wars have been fought over dinosaurs, but between 1870 and 1900 a battle raged in the midwestern United States. Two rival paleontologists, Edward Cope and Othniel Marsh, fought to make new finds, spending huge amounts of money on field crews. They named nearly all the famous American dinosaurs: *Allosaurus*, *Apatosaurus*, *Camarasaurus*, *Camptosaurus*, *Ceratosaurus*, *Diplodocus*, *Nodosaurus*, *Ornithotarsus*, *Stegosaurus*, and *Triceratops*. Their battles have been called the "Bone Wars."

Marsh

Cope

Diplodocus

Mamenchisaurus

Styracosaurus

The giant sauropods had very strong backbones. In some, the vertebrae were welded together. This gave an anchor for the muscles and ligaments holding up the body and the massive tail.

Heavy names

The big sauropods have names that tell us how big they were. First there was *Cetiosaurus*, or "whale lizard," then *Brontosaurus*, or "thunder lizard." More recently, some even larger sauropods have come to light, *Supersaurus*, or "higher lizard" in 1971, *Ultrasaurus*, or "even higher lizard" in 1979, and *Seismosaurus*, or "earth shaking lizard" in 1989. What name could be invented for the next even bigger dinosaur to be found? Can you think of one?

17

TEMPERATURE CONTROL

One of the great debates in recent years has been whether the dinosaurs were cold-blooded or warm-blooded. Were they really just cold-blooded animals like modern fish and reptiles, whose body temperatures are the same as the surrounding air or water? Or could they keep a constant warm body temperature, like modern birds and mammals? The answer remains unclear. All that can be said is that the dinosaurs were probably somewhere in between. If this is the case, it could explain why dinosaurs were so successful. A constant body temperature would have allowed them to be active all of the time, not just when the air was warm. However, they would not have had to eat as much as true warm-blooded animals do; nine-tenths of what we eat is for body-heat control.

Polar dinosaurs
It was once thought that dinosaurs lived only in the warmer parts of the world, and this fit the idea that they were simply cold-blooded reptiles. However, recently, dinosaurs have been found in Alaska, in the Arctic Circle, and in southern Australia, which used to lie within the Antarctic Circle. The dinosaurs from Australia include *Hypsilophodon,* medium-sized plant-eaters known also from Europe and North America.

Hypsilophodon skeleton

Dimetrodon, an early mammal-like reptile, had a "fin" that took up the morning heat quickly and acted as a cooling radiator when the body was too hot.

Stegosaurus had blood vessels in the skin over its bony plates. Heat was taken in and given off.

Dimetrodon

Warming up
In the morning, reptiles stand out in the sun and soak up the heat. This is called basking. Some fossil reptiles had special devices to help them do this faster. Some mammal-like reptiles had fins made from bony spines and skin, and the plant-eating dinosaur *Stegosaurus* had skin-covered bony plates.

Cooling down

Modern reptiles take shelter when they become too hot. In the midday heat, they hide behind rocks. Dinosaurs may have used their fins, spines, and skin to give off heat, or they may have curled up on the ground in some shade and stopped moving altogether until they cooled down.

Stegosaurus

Dinosaurs were probably cold-blooded, just like modern reptiles. But most of them were so big that they were as good as warm-blooded. In other words, they took so long to warm up in the morning and to cool down at night, that their body temperatures were nearly constant.

Mathematical dinosaurs

Experiments with living alligators have shown that small ones have the same body temperature as the air around them. Large alligators, weighing 220 pounds, have more constant body temperatures, even when the days are hot and the nights are cold. So, a dinosaur weighing 10 tons or more is likely to have kept the same body temperature day or night, simply because it was so big.

The new dinosaur artists

Early pictures of dinosaurs made them look like rhinoceroses. Since 1850, however, dozens of artists have used all their skills to illustrate what scientists have found out about the life of the dinosaurs. In 1968, some exciting drawings by a new dinosaur artist, Robert Bakker, were published in the United States. These showed dinosaurs as active, lively animals, running with their backs level, and not standing up like kangaroos.

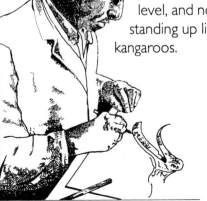

DISPLAYING AND EGG-LAYING

Did dinosaurs live in families, and how did they talk to each other? How did they lay their eggs? New work in North America and in Mongolia has shown that dinosaurs were able to pass complex signals to each other, partly through sight, and partly through sound. The males and females often looked quite different from each other. The males seem to have had larger horns and crests which they may have used in fighting for mates, and for displaying, just as with deer and antelope today. After the males and females had paired off, the mothers made large nests in the ground, and laid their eggs. It seems that dinosaur societies were probably just as complicated as any mammal community today.

Males and females

Some of the biggest differences between males and females are seen among the plant-eating, duckbilled dinosaurs, like *Corythosaurus, Parasaurolophus,* and *Tsintaosaurus.* When many skeletons are found together, half of them may have tall crests, and the other half smaller crests. The horned dinosaurs, like *Triceratops,* also seem to show differences in the length of the horns over their eyes. The horns of the meat-eater *Ceratosaurus* may have been larger in males, who probably used them to establish territory.

Dinosaurs laid ten to thirty eggs at a time, often arranged in regular circles, in an earth nest on the ground. They covered the nest with leaves and mud to protect the eggs. After a few weeks the young hatched out. Some parent dinosaurs then fed the young after hatching (see pages 22-23).

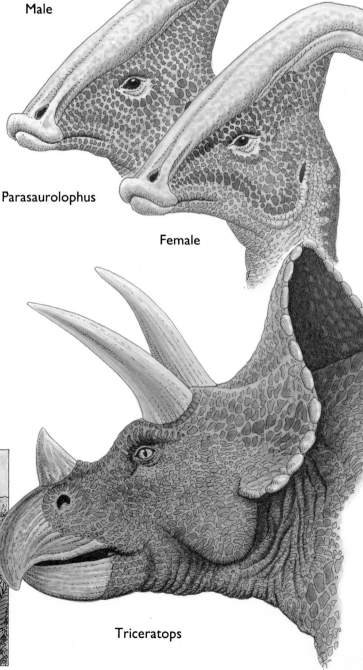

Male

Parasaurolophus

Female

Triceratops

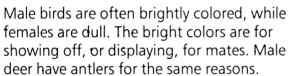

Male birds are often brightly colored, while females are dull. The bright colors are for showing off, or displaying, for mates. Male deer have antlers for the same reasons.

Corythosaurus

John Sibbick

One of the best-known modern dinosaur artists is John Sibbick. He painted a series of pictures of all the major dinosaurs for a 1985 book, and he is now one of the most famous dinosaur painters.

Tsintaosaurus

Musical crests

Inside the crests of the duckbills, air passages were found linking the nostrils to the throat. When air passes through a tube, it causes it to vibrate, producing sound waves. Try blowing down a long, coiled tube. This is how trumpets produce sound. When these dinosaurs puffed out hard, they whistled and produced trumpeting sounds.

Ceratosaurus

HAPPY FAMILIES?

Dinosaurs have had bad press in the past. Until recently, many people thought that the dinosaurs must have been blood-thirsty monsters. They believed that dinosaurs were so horrible that they would have eaten their own babies! This idea came from stories brought back by explorers in Africa over a hundred years ago. They claimed to have seen crocodile mothers eating their babies as they hatched out of their eggs. However, new studies show that the mother crocodiles are actually scooping up the tiny babies in their mouths, and carrying them down to the water for safety. Dinosaur digs in North America have now shown that these great reptiles also took care of their young, feeding the babies and protecting them from meat-eaters.

Iguanodon family

The Victorians

In Victorian times, 100 years ago, reptiles were said to be slimy, cold, and evil. In the Bible, it is a snake in the Garden of Eden that tempts Adam and Eve to become wicked. It is not surprising, then, that they thought dinosaurs were also horrible, cruel monsters. Old pictures often show dinosaurs as ferocious-looking sea creatures.

Dinosaurs lived in family groups, with babies, young ones, and adults, together. This has been shown by some of the new dinosaur digs around nest sites. Eggs and babies are found in the nests, surrounded by the bodies of one- and two-year olds, mothers, and fathers.

Cloning dinosaurs

Can you imagine what it would be like if dinosaurs were alive today? Steven Spielberg's film *Jurassic Park*, based on the book by Michael Crichton, might give you some idea. Scientists clone (duplicate) DNA, the basic building block of life, from fossilized dinosaur-biting insects. In real life, scientists in England and Holland did extract dinosaur proteins in 1992. Some day DNA may be found in dinosaur bone, but it does not seem likely that it will ever be possible to clone this to make a living dinosaur.

Walking, talking dinosaurs?

The best chance to see a "living" dinosaur is in a museum. The new dinosaur "robots," made from latex and steel, show lifelike movements and sounds. Many of them are based on hours of study of clues in the bones and in the rocks. Then, huge amounts of time are spent building the intricate electronic equipment inside that makes them move their arms and legs, blink their eyes, and open their mouths to roar. Engineers and artists at the Tokyo-based company *Kokoro* are pioneers in the development and animation of dinosaur models. Their models are supplied to theme parks and museums around the world. The company uses the latest scientific research. Workshop artists sculpt polyurethane bodies over pneumatically driven metal skeletons. Then, they texture and paint the silicone rubber skin. No one knows what colors dinosaurs were, but scientists guess that their colors were as varied as those of today's birds.

Some dinosaur babies were able to get out of the nest right after hatching. They could trot about and find scraps of food right away. Others, however, had to stay in the nest for a few weeks or months. They were helpless, and had to be fed with soft plants brought back by a parent, or even by a big brother or sister.

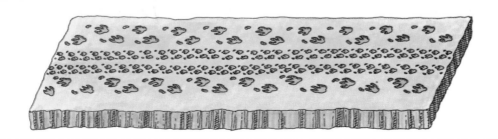

Some dinosaur tracks show that the parents protected their babies when they were moving. The small tracks are in the middle, and the larger ones on the outside.

DEFENSE

Most dinosaurs were plant-eaters, and therefore had to fear attacks from the great meat-eaters. Only the giant sauropods were big enough not to have any enemies. Meat-eaters hunted with their huge clawed feet, massive jaws, and razor-sharp slashing claws. Some plant-eaters saved themselves by being able to run very fast. But others had to be able to defend themselves. The armor-plated ankylosaurs were almost completely protected, and some of them had tails like clubs which they could use to hit an attacker. The rhinoceros-like ceratopsians used their nose and forehead horns to attack. The meat-eaters were not able to have it all their own way!

Deinonychus had a fearsome killing claw on each foot. It lifted the attacking leg back, and flicked the claw up and back. Then, it swept the claw across the side of the body of a plant-eater, swinging the claw down in a great tearing slash.

Fact meets fiction

Since their first discovery, dinosaurs have featured in fiction. Some of the greatest science fiction writers wrote books about time travel. A typical example was *The Lost World* by Sir Arthur Conan Doyle (1859-1930), the inventor of the great detective Sherlock Holmes. In *The Lost World*, Professor Challenger leads an expedition to South America where he finds living dinosaurs in a forgotten upland area. Other famous science fiction books that feature dinosaurs are: *A Journey to the Center of the Earth* by Jules Verne (1828-1905), and *The Land that Time Forgot* by the author and creator of *Tarzan*, Edgar Rice Burroughs (1875-1950).

Arthur Conan Doyle

Triceratops

Triceratops was a plant-eater, but it was well able to fight off *Tyrannosaurus* by using its horns to pierce the meat-eater's belly.

Nodosaurus

Tyrannosaurus rex, the biggest meat-eating animal of all time, was a fearsome predator. It used its huge birdlike feet to kick at prey animals and to hold them down while tearing the flesh with its massive jaws. Tyrannosaurus had such tiny arms that the hands could not reach its mouth.

T-rex

The thumb spike

The first plant-eating dinosaur to be found was Iguanodon. A large pointed bone was found with the early skeletons, and scientists at the time thought it was a nose horn. Later, it became clear that the "nose horn" was, in fact, a thumb claw. Perhaps it was used to slash at attackers.

Dinosaur films

The first dinosaur film using models was made in 1914. Early films are well-known for their unrealistic and often amusing animation techniques. "Stop-frame" animation using rubber models resulted in a jerky, unrealistic motion. Another alternative was to stick "dinosaur fins" onto the backs of real lizards. Since then, dozens of films have been made, and the models have become better and better.

Armor plating

The ankylosaurs look like harmless turtles, with their all-over covering of armor plates. However, many ankylosaurs were absolutely huge, the size of army tanks. Their armor was a good defense against predatory meat-eaters.

Pinacosaurus

Euoplocephalus

INTELLIGENCE

The most popular view of dinosaurs – apart from being big – is that they were stupid. It is often said that dinosaurs had no brains at all, or that their brains were too small for their bodies. The idea is that they were so stupid, they simply could not survive sufficiently and eventually died out. This is not quite true. It would be wrong to suggest that dinosaurs were highly intelligent, but their brains were the right size for reptiles, and some even had bird-sized brains. How can paleontologists tell how bright a dinosaur was, when they all died out so long ago? The first clue comes from the size of the brain, and that can be measured by looking at the size of the skull.

Top of the class

The brainiest dinosaur was a small one called *Saurornithoides*, which lived 75 million years ago in Mongolia. It was a thin 6 feet long animal, but its brain was as big as a bird's. It has been suggested that they were about as brainy as modern emus, and more intelligent than any modern reptiles. They were meat-eaters with a killing claw on the foot.

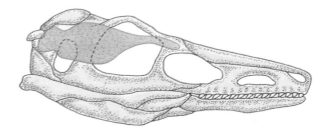

Saurornithoides' brain
(shown in blue)

Saurornithoides

How brainy?

Intelligence depends on the size of the brain in proportion to the body size. So, in a small dinosaur like *Saurornithoides*, the brain is relatively big. *Stegosaurus* on the other hand had the same size of brain, but its body was much, much bigger. It was probably one of the most stupid dinosaurs. Think about modern animals. Whales and elephants have bigger brains than humans, but their bodies are much larger too. So, intelligence does not necessarily increase with brain size.

Dinosaur = failure

The word "dinosaur" is often used in everyday speech to mean a failure, something that is old-fashioned, too big, and not able to change. This is based on assumptions that the dinosaurs were much too big to survive, and that they died out because they were hopeless and useless. In fact, the dinosaurs were very successful; after all, they ruled the Earth for 165 million years, much longer than the mammals have so far. They lived all over the Earth, in many habitats, growing much larger than any mammal.

A human dinosaur?

What if the dinosaurs had not died out? How would they have evolved? A Canadian paleontologist, Dr. Dale Russell, tried to imagine what might have happened. He chose one of the brightest dinosaurs, *Stenonychosaurus*, a relative of *Saurornithoides*, as his starting point. This dinosaur lived about 70 million years ago, just before their end. He thought it would evolve to be fully upright, and that it would lose its tail. Also, its brain would have become larger, and it would have developed hands that were even better at grasping. In fact, a model of "dinosauroid" looks very much like a lizardy human being!

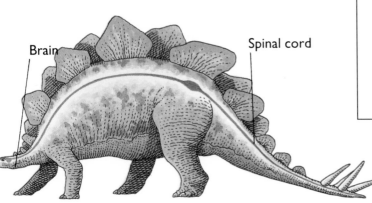

Brain

Spinal cord

Stegosaurus

It is sometimes said that *Stegosaurus* had a brain in its bottom, and that this was larger than the real brain in its head. In fact, the second "brain" is simply a swelling in the spinal cord.

Measuring brain power

Intelligence can be measured by comparing brain size with body size. When this is done for modern animals, reptiles turn out to have much lower intelligence than birds or mammals. Dinosaurs had typical reptile intelligence, although some were as bright as birds.

Cast of a dinosaur brain

Troödon is a relative of *Saurornithoides,* and another small-sized brainy dinosaur. These dinosaurs chased small animals at speed, twisting and turning. This needed good eyesight and balance, and a good brain.

EXTINCTION

The most intriguing question about dinosaurs has always been "why did they die out?" There is no simple answer to this question, even though many hundreds of scientists are studying the problem. They are not studying the extinction of the dinosaurs alone, but the whole question of extinction. Many other plants and animals have died out in the past, and it is important to understand how and why this happened. Having this information could help save many species that are under threat in the modern world. Humans are causing extinctions now, because of pollution and other damage to the environment. Maybe clues about the dinosaurs can tell us how to save the Earth today, because of their extinction 65 million years ago!

Early ideas
Some of the early dinosaur scientists, 100 years ago, thought the dinosaurs died out because the air changed, and they could not breathe. Others thought that the dinosaurs disappeared simply because they became too big. They were too heavy to move without falling over, and could not find enough food to survive.

One theory is that a huge killer meteorite hit the Earth. Smaller meteorites have fallen since then, making craters like this one in Arizona.

Survivors
Whatever happened 65 million years ago, most plants and animals were not wiped out. Among the reptiles, the crocodiles, turtles, tortoises, lizards, and snakes survived. So too did the mammals, birds, amphibians, fish, and most plants and sea creatures.

Tortoise

Crocodile

Perhaps huge amounts of lava poured out of volcanoes in India. This sent up vast clouds of dust that blacked out the sun, and made the Earth icy cold.

Dinosaurs and people in films

A lot of dinosaur films in the past have shown people and dinosaurs living at the same time. There are often epic battles between spear-waving cavemen and dinosaurs. No human being, however, could have wrestled with a dinosaur, since the dinosaurs died out 60 million years before the first humans lived!

Evidence from fossil leaves (above) shows that climates became colder. Perhaps that was enough to kill off the dinosaurs?

The final curtain

Dinosaurs were not the only animals to die out 65 million years ago. The flying pterosaurs also disappeared, as did the swimming plesiosaurs and some other reptile groups and shellfish in the sea. Many other plants and animals, however, did survive, and life on Earth had returned to "normal" about 10 million years later. "Normality," of course, also meant a world without the dinosaurs. 160 million years of domination by these beasts had ended.

Measuring rates of extinction

You've probably heard the expression "dead as a Dodo." The Dodo is just one of millions of species of plants and animals that have died out. Extinction is quite normal. However, sometimes so many species die out all at the same time that something unusual must have been going on. One of these mass extinctions happened when the dinosaurs died out.

Dodo

DISCOVERING DINOSAURS

1677

The first dinosaur bone was illustrated in a book. Robert Plot (left), Professor of Chemistry at Oxford University, described part of a huge thighbone that had been dug up nearby. He thought it came from a giant person. It turned out later to be part of *Megalosaurus*.

1824

The first dinosaur was named scientifically. *Megalosurus*, was announced by Dean William Buckland of Oxford University.

1825

The second dinosaur to be named was announced by Gideon Mantell. *Iguanodon* was named after some teeth and limb bones.

1842

The group *Dinosauria* was named by Professor Richard Owen. He recognized, for the first time, that the giant reptiles were not lizards, but belonged to a special group of their own.

1853

The Crystal Palace dinosaurs were built by Waterhouse Hawkins and exhibited in London. These were the first life-sized models of dinosaurs.

1858

The first complete dinosaur skeleton was unearthed in North America. It was a duckbilled dinosaur named *Hadrosaurus*, found by Joseph Leidy.

1861

Discovery of *Archaeopteryx* (below), the world's oldest bird. Recognized later as a missing link between dinosaurs and birds.

1878

Discovery of a herd of *Iguanodon* in a coal mine at Bernissart in Belgium. Dozens of skeletons that had become trapped in a sand bank were found.

1887

Discovery of the first remains of the horn-faced dinosaur *Triceratops*. This was one of the dozens of dinosaurs collected by Edward Cope and Othniel Marsh, sworn enemies.

1902

The first skeletons and skulls of *Tyrannosaurus rex* were excavated in Montana, by Barnum Brown.

1909-11

The biggest dinosaur dig ever at Tendaguru in East Africa, involving 500 workers each year.

Many spectacular Jurassic dinosaurs were dug up, including *Brachiosaurus*, the biggest of all.

1923

The first discoveries of dinosaurs from Mongolia, and nests of the early horn-faced dinosaur *Protoceratops*.

1979

Discovery of *Ultrasaurus* supposedly the world's largest dinosaur, by Jim Jensen (right) in Colorado.

1983

Discovery of *Baryonyx*, the sickle-clawed meat-eater from the Early Cretaceous in Surrey, England.

1987

Discovery of the first dinosaur skeleton in Antarctica, the only continent which had never yielded a dinosaur bone.

1993

The discovery of *Eoraptor* (below) in Argentina by Paul Sereno. The world's most primitive dinosaur, dating from the Triassic, 230 million years ago.

GLOSSARY

Amphibians Backboned animals that live on dry land, but must return to the water to breed.

Bacterium (plural, bacteria) One of the simplest living things; a single-celled creature.

Cloning Making copies of a cell or cell type by growing it on a suitable supply of food.

Community The animals and plants that live together in a particular place or habitat.

Continental drift Change in the layout of the Earth's surface by movement of the plates that support the Earth's lands and oceans.

DNA Abbreviation for deoxyribose nucleic acid, the chemical in all living things that codes information to control their development.

Era An interval of geological time, comprising several periods.

Extinction The disappearance, or dying out, of a species or other group.

Fossil The remains of a plant or animal that once lived, usually preserved in rock.

Geology The study of the Earth, its history and the processes that shape it.

Habitat The surroundings in which a plant or animal lives, including plant life, other animals, physical landscape, and climate.

Ligament Tough ropelike strands that help to support parts of the skeleton.

Mammal-like reptiles The large group of reptiles that were important in the 100 million years before the dinosaurs. Includes the ancestors of the mammals.

Mammals Hairy, backboned animals.

Migration Animals moving, often over long distances, from one part of the Earth to another.

Mineral A part of a rock. A pure chemical usually in a solid, hard form.

Omnivore An animal that eats both animal and plant material.

Pelvis The hipbones of a skeleton, resting on the legs and supporting the spine.

Paleontologist A person who studies fossils.

Radioactivity The breakdown, or decay, of certain chemical substances that are present in an unstable state. Radioactivity, a special form of energy, is given off while the decay takes place.

Reptiles The scaly, land-living, backboned animals. Modern forms include turtles, lizards, snakes, and crocodiles. The fossil forms include dinosaurs and pterosaurs.

Skeleton The structure, made from bones, that forms a framework for the body, supporting the muscles.

Species A group of very similar plants and animals that are all closely related. All human beings are one species, while all dogs are another.

Territory The area in which an animal or group of animals lives, and which it defends against intruders.

Vertebrae The individual bones that form the segments of the backbone.

Virus One of the simplest living things. A single-celled creature that lives largely by entering and feeding in the bodies of larger creatures.

INDEX

Photocredits
ABBREVIATIONS: T-top, M-middle, B-bottom, L-left, R-right
Cover & pages 4t, 5, 6b,16b & 21b: Roger Vlitos; 2, 10t, 23 & 28t: Science Photo Library; 3, 25b & 29t: BFI Stills, Posters & Designs; 4b, 15r, 16t, 22 both & 28b: Mary Evans Picture Library; 6t, 10m & b, 12, 13, 14, 15, 20, 21t, 24, 25t, 26 & 27: The Natural History Museum, London; 8, 16m, 28m & 29b: Bruce Coleman Ltd.